SCIENCE AND THE BIBLE
Can we believe both?

Larry Richards

Contents

1. Either/or? **3**
2. Puzzle-solving **6**
3. The big picture **9**
4. With authority **12**
5. Foul! **15**
6. Miracles **18**
7. Creation vs. organic evolution **21**
8. The Genesis flood **24**
9. What's new? **27**
10. The test **30**

ISBN 0-88207-372-9

Published by
VICTOR BOOKS
a division of SP Publications, Inc.

© 1973, SP Publications, Inc. World rights reserved.
Printed in the United States of America

1
Either/or?

"Of course," Professor Carlson was saying, "hardly anyone these days takes such primitive myths seriously."

"I do!"

Carl was jolted by the sound of his own voice. What a way to start off your first course in college science! Just because the prof doesn't believe the Bible, a guy needn't make an issue of it.

"Really?" Dr. Carlson was looking right at him, sorting through the class cards to find his name. "Mr. Stinson?"

"Yes, sir," Carl admitted miserably, wishing he could just fall through the floor.

"You actually believe in the Bible?" the professor asked, with what seemed to Carl amused amazement. Carl nodded unhappily. "Well, Carl, I certainly appreciate your willingness to stand up for your beliefs. But I hope that through this semester we can help you get beyond what you've been taught. Modern science has made it perfectly clear that the things your Bible teaches just couldn't be. Thanks to science, we know a lot more than Moses did!

"But let's get back to our main point this morning. We want to think about science as man's primary and most successful road to knowledge and control of our environment . . ."

In conflict?
We often share Carl's embarrassment when we're confronted

by friends or teachers who say that "science" has disproven Scripture, and made Bible teachings (such as Creation, the Flood, miracles, heaven and hell) ridiculous.

Yet, how can we answer a person who claims confidently that science has made the Bible outdated and disproven its "primitive" beliefs? Is there any answer? Or do we have to choose between science and Scripture? Must we either accept a scientific ("educated" and "respectable") view of the world, or, against all the evidence, hold to our biblical ("ignorant" and "primitive") thinking? This isn't an easy choice to make! Especially when guys and gals in high school and college actually face just such challenges to their faith.

But is it an either/or choice? Actually, most people who claim with that superior smile that "science" has disproven the Bible know very little about the Bible . . . or about science! Others who think that the Bible and science are in conflict have badly distorted ideas about science. For instance, take this true/false quiz, and see how much *you* know about science.

___1. Scientific evidence proves evolution happened.
___2. Natural laws discovered by science make the possibility of miracles very very remote.
___3. The "scientific method" can be applied to find out things about the past or future as well as the present.
___4. Science is the way modern man discovers Truth.
___5. The findings of modern science have made the Bible's statements seem ever more primitive.
___6. The scientist holds his beliefs on "evidence" rather than faith.
___7. Scientists are better qualified than others to speak about the origin of the world and of man.
___8. "Science" may be thought of as a body of truth that has grown over hundreds of years without any drastic changes of thought or belief.

Maybe it will surprise you, but each of these statements is false. *And scientists (not theologians) are the people who say they're false!* Yet, it's on the basis of just such naïve and false notions about science that people talk so glibly about science "disproving" the Bible.

Not either/or

A Christian doesn't need to apologize to science for believing the Bible.

Sure, there are scientists who don't believe the Bible and who talk of it as primitive. But let's not confuse what some *scientists* believe with "what science teaches" or "what science says." There's a big difference! Some scientists may believe in evolution and present scientific evidence for their conviction. But there are many scientists who believe the Bible!

Hundreds of scientists have banded together in the Creation Research Society, which publishes a scholarly journal edited by Dr. John N. Moore, professor of natural sciences at Michigan State University, to present *scientific evidence* showing the credibility of the Bible's teaching about Creation.

Another organization of scientists who are Christians and believe the Bible is the American Scientific Affiliation. It publishes a scholarly journal (edited by Dr. Richard Bube, professor of materials science at Stanford University) that presents a wide spectrum of viewpoints on the relation of science and Scripture.

So "science" is appealed to by both sides. It's not an "either/or" situation. It's not either science, or the Bible.

Then why do so many people take it for granted that science is against the Bible? *Washington Evening Star-Daily News* columnist William Willoughby[1] filed suit in 1972 in the United States District Court against the state of Virginia for a one-sided presentation of the evolutionist view in the schools. He didn't ask that the schools stop teaching evolution. But he did complain that "by *excluding* a theory (Creation) that is just as plausible as the evolution theory, school children grow up believing the evolution theory is the only way thinkable." Perhaps this is why so many people think that "science" has "disproven" the Bible. They've never even heard the other side. A side that we want to look at now.

---

1. In "Washington Perspective," Saturday, August 12, 1972, *The Evening Star-Daily News,* Washington, D.C.

2 Puzzle-solving

Dr. Thomas S. Kuhn,[1] in *The Structure of Scientific Revolutions,* has called "normal science" puzzle-solving. It seems funny, and suggests putting the scientist alongside a lady working a crossword as she rides the bus to a downtown sale. But it helps clear away a lot of fuzzy thinking.

T. H. Huxley[2] once illustrated the nature of scientific investigation with the story of a man who bites into a hard, green apple, and finds it bitter. Later he tries another. It's bitter too. So he develops the notion that hardness and greenness in apples is associated with bitterness. If he wants to see if this notion is a "law" (a true general statement of the way things really are) he tests it in a number of ways. He gets apples from different parts of the world. He talks with people who know apples. He keeps biting into hard, green apples. If all these lines of investigation show that hard, green apples are bitter, he becomes more and more confident that he's discovered a "law of nature."

All scientific inquiry uses this basic method (observation, verification) to establish laws or principles. These give rise to other notions, which are themselves tested to see if they can be verified, and so on. In the process, our understanding of the universe (at least that which can be observed and tested) grows.

---

1. U. of Chicago Press, 1970, pp. 35-42
2. In "the method of scientific investigation" from "Darwiniana"

The hard, green sweet apple
But let's suppose that, after biting 10,000 hard, green bitter apples, the man bites one hard, green, *sweet* apple. Does he throw out the "law"? Not yet. No, he has a puzzle: an apple that doesn't fit what he knows about apples. *Why* isn't *this* hard, green apple bitter like the rest of them? What makes it different? How can he explain it? Fascinated by the puzzle, he may try to think of explanations, and then test these explanations to see if one of them is right.

This is what Dr. Kuhn means about normal science being puzzle-solving. Science is always trying to understand things that don't quite fit what we know about the world in general, and so to learn more.

This form of inquiry (the "scientific method") has proven unbelievably successful in helping us deal with the physical universe. We've learned to send radio and TV signals from earth to moon and back. We've been able to harness atomic energy and meter its release so that it operates a pacemaker to regulate the heartbeat of a cardiac patient who otherwise would die. As Dr. Warren Weaver, longtime director of the Division of Natural Sciences of the Rockefeller Foundation, has noted, "There seems to be no inherent limitation to the distance science can penetrate, no limit to the amount of experience that can be explained and brought under control by the methods of science."

Strength, and weakness
It's pretty hard not to stand back in awe when we consider the tremendous ability of the scientific method to give the knowledge and provide the technology that makes our modern world. It's even harder to realize that science's great strength is also its great weakness.

What I mean is this.

Science operates by *observation* and *experimentation*. Every notion the scientist develops must be verified. Does water boil at 212°F.? Let's boil a potful and see. Let's do it again and again, to see if it happens regularly. When we've verified a thing by experiment, then and then only do we feel that "we know."

But wait. You may have noticed I just made an incorrect statement. It's *not entirely true* to say that "water boils at 212°

F." Anyone who lives in Denver can contradict that "law." For Denver is the "mile high" city . . . over 5,000 feet above sea level. If our scientist tries his experiment there, he finds that water boils *before* is reaches 212°F. Observing this difference, the scientist tries to explain it:

"When I first boiled water, I was in Los Angeles. What's the difference between Los Angeles and Denver? Well, Los Angeles is at sea level. Maybe the higher one goes (and the fewer pounds per square inch of air pressure), the lower water's boiling point."

This notion too can be tested. Boil water at different altitudes. When it *is* tested, we learn enough to restate the "law" accurately: "water boils at 212°F. *at sea level.*"

So you see? Scientists depend on observation and experiment to gather their information in the first place, *and* scientists depend on observation and experiment to correct their inadequate notions . . . if you will, their half-truths. *Where there is no possibility of verification by observation and experimentation, "science" has no way to speak with authority.*

Now, think for a moment about the idea that "science" has "disproven" the Bible's teaching about Creation. *How* did "science" disprove it? Did a scientist observe earth's origination? Have scientists rerun "the beginning" (as water was boiled over and over again) to correct and test their notions? Of course not!

Scientists have *speculated* on what the earth's early conditions *might* have been and then used observation and experimentation under these conditions to see what might have happened. This is hardly scientific proof of what *did* happen. The very method and strength of science (its insistence that we *must* gain information about the universe by observation and experimentation) makes it utterly impossible that there can be "scientific proof" for or against *either* evolution or Creation.

3
The big picture

Before we go much further we have to pause and pay attention to an outraged cry from some scientists. "Talk about half-truths!" they might shout indignantly. *"You just presented a half-truth by implying that we can only speak out on small, discrete things (like water boiling) and not on whole systems!"*

We have to listen to this objection: it's a fair one. The scientist cares about the little observations *because* they help him build bigger pictures of the universe. The discovery that water boils at 212°F. at sea level isn't immensely important *in itself*. It's important as one more bit of information that, added to other bits, lets the scientist understand more about liquids and pressures *as a whole*.

Here the scientist who presents evolution as a "fact" and ignores Creation as a primitive myth feels on more solid ground. "Technically," he might say, "it is true that we cannot *know* about evolution or creation. But we put the facts we have together. This way we can build a pretty accurate picture of what happened, even if we can't, strictly speaking, 'know' it." So the secular man still wants to claim *science* has given him his information, and that it's because of science that he rejects the Bible.

But it's important to note something here. "Science" is a way of gathering and verifying information. The way we interpret that information is *not* "science," strictly speaking. It's *reasoning.* And it is entirely possible that we may reason to a false conclusion from scientific facts.

So we need to ask whether scientists have ever reasoned incorrectly from scientific information? And do established facts themselves rule out things the Bible teaches?

Revolution!

This is how Dr. Thomas Kuhn[1] sees the many and jolting changes in scientific outlooks. Not only have the ideas of scientists about things as a whole changed: they have changed in every scientific field!

Newtonian physics was a complete overhaul of the physics before John Newton. Within 60 years, Europe's best mathematical physicists were aware that his picture of the universe gave rise to many puzzles: for instance, the predicted motion of the moon's perigee was only half what they observed. But though many facts didn't fit, scientists continued to view the world in a Newtonian framework until Einstein's theory of relativity and Heisenberg's work on quantum mechanics provided a *new* picture . . . a picture of nonmaterial atoms and random motion that fit the observed facts better than the idea of a "solid" reality of mass and motion. The same thing has happened in chemistry, in optics, in the study of gasses—in every field. Scientists have reasoned incorrectly from the facts to broader theories that have later proven false or inadequate.

The scientist may well reply that this shows how consistently science tends to be self-correcting. After all, it is the scientist who discovers information that tends to support or to discredit any theory.

With this, we must agree. But this pattern of change still gives us every reason to consider scientific theories *as theories,* not facts.

The point is simply this. (1) Scientists always try to develop broad theories that explain or "fit" the facts they observe. Evolution is an example of such a theory. (2) The history of science has included many wrong or inadequate guesses from fact to theory. This process of "handling the same bundle of data as

---

1. Op. cit.

before, but placing them in a new system of relationships with one another," [2] is normal and natural in science. *So every scientific theory is tentative; something to be used to help us put together what we know until we see a better way of putting it together.* (3) Scientific revolutions [replacing of old "big pictures" with new ones] are resisted and, as Dr. Kuhn points out, tend to happen only when so many puzzles appear that everyone realizes the old theory just won't work anymore. (4) As long as there are serious puzzles . . . significant bits of scientific data that do not fit a theory . . . no one can honestly say that a theory is "proved."

So?

It's clear that scientists *have* often reasoned incorrectly from scientic data, and that no broad theory can be presented as "scientific truth." Not if we're honest. A scientist can say, "I think my picture of evolution is better than your picture of creation." But he cannot say "science has proven evolution and disproved the Bible."

The conflict between the Bible and science isn't such a conflict at all! As Stanford University science professor Dr. R. Bube[3] has said, "Every time there is an apparent contradiction between science (a system of interpreting nature) and theology (a system of interpreting the Bible), it must be because one or both systems of interpretation are in error." It's not science that conflicts with the Bible. Rather, the scientist's *interpretation* of his facts may conflict with the Bible, or the Christian's *interpretation* of his Bible may conflict with the facts.

---

2. Dr. Warren Weaver, "The Imperfections of Science" from "Proceedings of the American Philosophical Society."
3. In "The Encounter Between Christianity and Science," Wm. B. Eerdmans, 1958.

4
With authority

Let's go back to Carl now, as he squirms under the condescending and authoritative pronouncements of his professor. "Modern science," Dr. Carlson was saying, "has made it clear that such things as your Bible describes just can't be."

Is the professor right? No . . . wrong! First, *science* is essentially a way of gathering information by observation and experimentation. The very method of science makes it impossible for science to speak authoritatively about origins, or the possibility of events such as miracles or the Flood. Second, while men have reasoned from information gathered by science to develop theories about the nature of things, we can never say that *science* has "proven" any theory. History has shown scientific theories to be short-lived and inadequate. As long as human reasoning is fallible; as long as we do not have *all* the facts; particularly as long as we have contradictory facts that simply won't fit an idea like evolution no matter how we push and pull them, we have no basis for the almost mystical confidence in evolution that many display. Or for the naïve assumption that *science* and the Bible are in conflict. Clearly, Dr. Carlson is out of line.

Limitations of science
While science has proven tremendously successful in dealing with physical nature, science has severe limitations. These limi-

tations, summarized by Dr. Warren Weaver,[1] are apparent to anyone who looks deeply within the system. "(1) He finds unresolved and apparently unresolvable disagreement among scientists concerning the relationship of scientific thought to reality —and concerning the very nature and meaning of reality itself. (2) He finds that the explanations of science have utility, but that they do in sober fact *not explain.* (3) He finds the old external appearance of inevitability completely vanished, for he discovers a charming capriciousness in all the individual events. (4) He finds that logic, so generally supposed to be infallible and unassailable, is in fact shaky and incomplete. (5) He finds that the whole concept of objective truth is a will-o-the-wisp."

For anyone who has been "deluded by external appearances and by partial understanding," Weaver continues, "into thinking of science as a relentless, all-conquering intellectual force, armed with finality and perfection, the limitations treated here would have to be considered damaging imperfections!" Science simply is *not* the authoritative and sure "last word" that it is popularly represented to be, as scientists themselves agree.

All this makes us wonder. How does being a scientist make a man an authority?

This is always a fair question. Say a guy runs a three-minute mile. Should we let him tell us how to vote? Does his athletic ability make him an authority on politics? In the same way we can wonder about scientists. Must we let them tell us about God and origins and miracles and the other things of which the Bible speaks? After all, a scientist, for all his skill in dealing with what he experiences in the physical universe, is not necessarily an authority on the *super*natural!

Of course, the Bible does claim that the supernatural has invaded, and affected, the natural world. So if any scientifically established facts, directly and in themselves, contradict specific Bible statements about the natural world, then we might feel we should pay attention to the scientist. He *can* speak with authority about verified facts of nature. But actually the scientifically established facts are *interpreted* differently by evolutionist and creationist. Each claims they support his point of view.

---

1. Op. cit.

So the scientist, as a scientist, has no more right or authority than the athlete to talk about "proving" or "disproving" the Bible. He has no valid claim to "know."

Beyond reasonable doubt

The phrase "beyond reasonable doubt" is often used in law. A jury is asked to look at evidence, and free or condemn a defendant. But if the jury members have a doubt *that they can assign a reason to,* the jury in our system is directed to find the defendant innocent.

This legal concept points up the problem with trying to "disprove" evolution *or* creation, or to "prove" either the scientific or biblical worldview. Both believers and unbelievers can give solid reasons for their convictions. Both can turn to scientifically established facts for support. Both can point out problems in the position taken by the other.

If we were to take "Evolution vs. Creation" into court and try the case on scientific evidence alone, the doctrine of reasonable doubt fairly applied would lead to a hung jury. Neither Evolution nor Creation would win.

Then why do men on both sides argue so vigorously and with such assurance? Why do some suggest that "science shows" evolution is true. And others that "science supports" the biblical view? To understand why men believe so firmly in things for which they simply do not have conclusive evidence, we have to leave the question of "science" and think about "faith." And we have to realize that the reason the scientist cannot be accepted as an authority who knows is that *his convictions rest as much on faith as does the Christian's conviction* that "in the beginning, God created . . . ."

5
Foul!

Most of us have a feeling for fair play. If you were playing a game of softball with the guys, you'd probably get uptight if you hit a ball over the centerfield fence and everyone on the other team yelled, "You're out." Out! It's a home run! No one can just change the rules of the game. That's not fair.

An unbelieving scientist may feel pretty much the same about the Christian's bringing God into things. Because the rules he plays his game by have no room for God.

Discovery
Earlier we saw that the method of science is to observe and experiment; to discover "laws" (like "hard, green apples are bitter") and to solve the puzzles that appear when something that's been accepted as a law doesn't seem to work.

Now, how does a scientist go about solving a puzzle? He proceeds on an unstated but utterly basic assumption: The solution to the problem will involve the discovery and application of laws of nature that were previously unknown or unapplied.

Think again of the boiling water from chapter three. Our scientist in Denver noted that it boils *before* the water temperature reaches 212°F. But why? He immediately begins casting about for an explanation. What's different about Denver from the place where water did boil (over and over) at 212°? Will this difference help explain what was observed? Once the scientist

15

latches on to the idea that altitude may make a difference, he tests it. He boils water at other high places, and finds that water *regularly* boils at a lower temperature at a higher altitude. Soon, by checking charts of air pressure at various altitudes, he is able to *predict* at just what temperature water will boil at the different altitudes. When his predictions work out (over and over), he's confident that he has discovered a regularity: a natural law. And he's solved the puzzle.

This rather simple illustration gives us much insight into the scientist's ground rules: the ways that science plays its game. (1) Science looks for regularity (laws) in nature. (2) When something that appears *irregular* shows up, he looks for some previously unknown regularity (a new law) to explain what puzzles him. (3) When he has discovered that new law, and proven that he knows how it works by predicting what will happen to things ruled by it, he has solved his puzzle and won his game.

The assumption that underlies this whole approach to nature and to knowing is this: *everything can be accounted for by natural laws operating within the physical universe.*

God?

Now perhaps you can see why science, as it has developed in our Western world, is suspicious of God . . . or at least indifferent to Him. Science plays it game *within nature,* and the whole point of the game is to explain what can be observed in nature by the discovery and application of natural laws.

Bringing God in just isn't fair! To say that the reason the 10,001st hard green apple was sweet is "God made it sweet" is not only nonsense by these rules . . . it's cheating! One simply doesn't play the game that way.

Here we have to agree with the scientist. *As far as his task is concerned,* (understanding the world we live in and helping men learn to control it), bringing God in is neither right nor helpful. After all, simply saying "God made the 10,001st apple sweet" is more likely to *keep us from trying to understand* than to help us probe for knowledge. But this is no problem for the Christian. We believe that God made the universe and controls it, but that (in general) He operates in the physical universe through the very laws and regularities the scientist cares about so passionately. Since God made the world regular and "lawful" . . . and as each of us profits from the scientist's discovery and application of His rules . . . we can appreciate and be thankful for the scientist's insistence on playing the game his way.

But . . .
The problem comes when the scientist insists that *his* game is the *only* game!

You see, it's quite all right for a scientist to say, "Let's go about science *as if* everything can and should be accounted for by natural laws operating within the physical universe." After all, the physical universe, with its laws and regularities, is the field on which the game of science is played. But when a scientist assumes that his rules apply to all of life and that his playing field is *all there is of reality,* then we object. He's no longer speaking of an operating assumption; he's giving a statement of faith.

Actually, the rules of any game apply only to the game they rule. You play softball by softball rules. For that game, the rules work well. But because softball rules work for softball is no reason to say, "There is no football!" So too, the rules of science work well when we're playing science. But when the game is over and we shower and leave the playing field, we leave the rules of that game behind. They no longer apply when it comes to talking about God, or the unobservable origins of the universe and life and man. Some scientists object, "But nature is all there is. There is no God." However, this is nothing more than a cry of "Foul!" from someone who, on faith and without evidence, conceives of his playing field as the whole of reality, and the rules of his game as the only rules for all.

6
Miracles

The scientist who objects most strenuously to miracles (as well as to a divine Creation and supernatural origin of man) does so because he believes that everything can and must be accounted for by the natural laws operating within the physical universe. Even a scientist who realizes the limitations of science, and so simply says, "I don't *know* about the supernatural," is likely to be upset by the notion of miracles.

Why? Because the Christian who talks about miracles (*un*-regular events in time and space that can not be explained by the discovery of unknown laws governing the physical universe) is stepping out on the scientist's own playing field. It's one thing to say that there is something beyond the physical universe; it's another thing entirely to assert that that "something beyond" acts in and on our world. This really must seem to the secular scientist to be cheating: a retreat to primitive days when men explained what they could not understand by appeal to some supernatural being.

Illegal?
This feeling that miracles are cheating, and somehow involve the breaking of natural law, is something the Christian can understand, but needn't agree with. For instance, we know that it's a "natural law" that rocks lay on the ground, held there by gravity. If a rock should tumble off a mountain ledge, it would

fall *down*. We might, rather simplistically, state as a general law, "rocks fall down or lay on the ground."

Now suppose that you're walking along the seashore and, picking up a rock, you throw it high in the air over a nearby sand dune. On the other side of the dune, a scientist glances up, and sees that rock curling *up* into the sky, and then falling down. *Would he conclude that somehow the rock broke a law of nature?* Not at all. The chances are he'd conclude, accurately, that someone beyond the dune picked up the rock and threw it. The actions of a person on the rock did not "break the law" at all. The actions of picking up and throwing the rock were simply the breaking in of animate nature (a living being) on inanimate nature (nonliving material), thus giving the inanimate bit of rock a force that caused it to fly. No laws were broken: the laws of inanimate nature were simply superseded by the higher laws and abilities of the animate.

Now, this is exactly what the Christian asserts of God and miracles. When God acts in the physical universe to cause an effect which cannot be explained by the rules under which the physical universe operates, He is not breaking laws; He is simply superseding them. A living person has greater freedom of action than a rock and is not completely bound by the natural laws that govern rocks. The Living God has infinitely greater freedom than man to act in this world He created!

Far from a breaking of natural law, miracles are simply one indication that there really is "someone over there beyond the dune." We can't see Him, but we can see the results of His actions.

Primitive beliefs?

This is what the secular scientist would like us to think—that in the old days people didn't know any better, and that's why they talked of miracles. That earlier peoples didn't understand, as the modern scientist does, such things as natural law and the regularity of nature.

But this notion is clearly wrong. If earlier people hadn't expected the world to behave in a regular, lawful way, how would they have identified the unusual as "miracles?" No, when Jesus healed the man born blind, everyone was amazed. When Jesus walked on the water, His disciples were startled and afraid.

When Jesus rose from the grave, and His resurrection was announced by those who first saw Him, even His closest friends couldn't bring themselves to believe it. These events were so unusual, such obvious miracles, that it seemed easier to doubt one's own eyes than to accept what they saw! Ultimately the disciples did accept the miracles . . . and they unashamedly reported them in the New Testament documents. Because by then they had come to know, in Jesus Christ, the God who had been there all the time, just over the dunes.

Retreat to faith

Both the believer and unbeliever, faced with miracles, respond with faith. The secular scientist asserts again, "It cannot be! *Everything* must be explained within the framework of the physical universe." And the Christian asserts, "It *can* be! For I know God, a God who made the physical universe, and who is free to act within it."

And at exactly this point, each of us must choose. What kind of universe *do* we live in? An impersonal, random one, that produced life and man by chance, and that dooms all life to blink out when the sun runs down and flickers out into eternal night? Or a personal one, with life that sprang from the hand of a God who loves each man and shapes the course of all things?

If we admit the possibility of the kind of God the Bible reveals, then "science" has no defense against miracles. And if you meet and come to know Jesus Christ who, being God, yet stepped into history, you'll find that the age of miracles isn't past! For even today God works His miracles, transforming the lives of those who trust in Christ and granting the answers to prayer so many Christians experience. Even today God is active, working all things for the good of those who love Him (Rom. 8:28).

7
Creation vs. organic evolution

Evolution is neither a new nor "scientific" theory. The first person known to propose it was Thales, a Greek philosopher hundreds of years before Christ who thought that men evolved from porpoises that had crawled out on the seashore and learned to walk. Just a hundred odd years ago, Charles Darwin's work gave rise to the modern theory that all life on earth is the result of processes growing out of the nature of things themselves. It's easy to see why this theory should be so quickly accepted. It fits the secular scientist's basic faith (that the rules of his game are the only rules) . . . even though there is no conclusive evidence for evolution, and even though there is serious question whether the mechanisms by which it could take place are tenable!

The evolutionary process
Simply stated, organic evolution means the gradual development of all forms of life by natural processes from a common ancestral form, which itself arose by natural processes from complex chemicals in the earth's primeval ocean. In Darwin's day, the idea of spontaneous generation of living from nonliving matter was widely accepted. Soon this idea was demolished by Pasteur and others. Yet scientists, rather than abandon their theory, turned to speculate about imagined conditions of atmosphere and ocean, and about processes that have no counterpart in today's world.

Darwin's explanation of evolution (natural selection) has long been rejected as the basic mechanism of change. Experiments with heredity have shown that the genes and chromosomes of all living matter provide for the variations Darwin first observed. But these variations operate within a fixed range. Thus natural selection, instead of tending to produce new species, really acts to preserve those that are already in existence!

But every other theory to explain evolution has also been shown to be inadequate. Jean Baptiste Lamarck, the French naturalist and pioneer in the field of comparative anatomy, suggested that characteristics acquired by one generation's *experience* were transmitted to the next. But soon scientists realized that the strength of the blacksmith is not automatically passed on as bulging muscles to his infant son, as Lamarck actually suggested.

The mutation theory of Hugo DeVries and others was based on observations of inheritable new characteristics that suddenly appeared in individuals. Yet all genuine mutations that have been observed are either neutral in character (they do not add to the survival potential of an organism), or are actually deadly. Moreover, the kind of mutations observed have *never* involved a change in species.

Other arguments

Often the evolutionist resorts to speaking of vast periods of time, over which the kinds of changes he proposes gradually occur. Yet the fossil record contains *no* transition forms between one kind and another.

Another line of "evolutionary evidence" is proposed from embryology. All animal embryos are similar at early stages, and develop along similar lines. Yet these visible similarities are hardly evidence of relationship or common origin. Especially when at every stage, examination of genes in cells unfailingly reveals the embryo's distinct species and character.

And we could go on. John Klotz, in his book *Genes, Genesis, and Evolution* (Concordia, 1955), has provided compelling and thoroughly documented evidence to show that processes and complexities within living things make the kind of changes evolution demands most unlikely. And such evidence is known, the puzzles recognized, by every scientist who troubles to note them.

Why then evolution?

The secular scientist has a faith to keep. A belief that everything *must* be explained within the framework of the natural universe. A faith that God does not exist, or, if He does, that He isn't the kind of God who meddles with His creation. And this faith some keep *against all the evidence.*

Now, none of this *proves* that God made all living things, and that, by a direct and special creation, God Himself formed man from the dust of the earth, and breathed into him the breath of life (Gen. 2:7). But the Christian who is confronted by the claim of the unbelieving scientist that "science has disproven the Bible" or that "evolution is proven" may be comforted to know that these are empty words. These words are a profession of faith and personal preference rather than a statement of fact.

Actually, the Christian can argue that the facts discovered by science fit creation better than evolution. Every discovery that presents some new objection to evolutionary theories is just what we might expect if creation really happened as described in God's word. And, thanks to the efforts of certain Christians who are also scientists, you can examine that evidence for yourself.

Yet, in the end, we too return to faith. "By faith . . . we know that the world and the stars—in fact, all things—were made at God's command; and that they were all made from things that can't be seen (Heb. 11:3, *Living Bible*). But how different our faith is from the evolutionists! We have faith because we have confidence in a God we've come to know in Jesus Christ. Our faith is no desperate effort to hold on to our presuppositions at any cost. That the facts of science fit our faith is no more or less than we expect.

8
The Genesis Flood

What we've called the "faith" of the secular scientist (his presupposition that we must explain everything we can observe by laws or principles operating within the physical universe) has also influenced geology. A theory called "uniformitarianism" assumes that all features of the earth's surface can be explained by presently observable processes, such as erosion, volcanic action, and sedimentation. This assumption seems to directly challenge the Scriptures. For the Bible, predicting a time when men would "scoff" and say "all things continue as they were from the beginning of the creation," reminds us that there was a day when God joltingly intervened to destroy by a great flood the world that then existed (2 Peter 3:3-6).

The Bible describes this flood as a cataclysm that swept over the whole earth, and destroyed all life except that which was saved in an ark built at God's invitation and command (cf. Gen. 6:17; 7:4-23; 9:11). Such a flood would certainly have left massive evidence. It would, in fact, have to account for most of the earth's great surface features and structures. Yet uniformitarianism stands opposed to a flood geology.

Evidence for uniformitarianism?
The uniformitarian idea is older than Darwin. It supposes several great periods of geologic prehistory (the Precambrian, Paleozoic, Mesozoic, and Cenozoic), during which rock forma-

tions were deposited. The notion is that, as the earth aged, rocks were formed and shaped all over the world in the same general sequence. Organic evolution is supposedly supported by discovery of fossil remains of less complex to more complex organisms in just that sequence of rocks. All this is presented in most earth science textbooks as observable fact. But it is misleading, to say the least.

The geologic column (formed by the accumulations of the millenia) is supposed to be about 100 miles deep (though the actual crust of the earth is about 10 miles deep). The column has been constructed theoretically, from rocks found all over the world, in layers never more than two miles or so deep. And the rocks themselves have sometimes been fitted into the column primarily *on the basis of the fossils found in them.* This is the most blatant kind of circular reasoning. It's like saying "tall girls are prettier than short girls," and then picking the tallest girl as prettiest because she's tall! When age is assigned to rocks by the fossils in them (not by mineral or lithographic qualities or relationship to strata above and below) *because* we've decided beforehand that the order we come up with must fit our theory of evolution, we have exactly the same situation.

The unexplained

We might forgive circular reasoning here if the rest of the observed facts fit uniformitarianism. But they don't! Instead, over and over again "older" rocks are found resting *on top of* "younger." Yet the *only reason* one strata is called "older" and the other "younger" is because the geologist and paleontologist presuppose that evolution is true and have so dated them by the fossils they contain!

At times such "upside down" rock strata can be explained by pressures on the earth's crust that have thrust some layers of rock over or between others. But often there is no evidence of such "faulting." Yet every mountain range in the world is known to have these "upside down" strata . . . something easily explained if the Bible's picture of the Flood is accepted, but inexplicable by uniformitarianism even if local catastrophies (in violation of the assumptions of the theory) are supposed to have caused them! You can read about the number and striking character of such inversions in a 518 page book by Dr. Henry M. Morris and Dr. John Whitcomb, *The Genesis Flood*. (Presbyterian and Reformed Publishing Co., $6.95, cloth, or Baker Book House, $1.95, paper.)

The cold truth

Siberia gives one instance of additional evidence of cataclysm. There, multitudes of mammoths have been found. In the north, where the ground is always frozen, preserved remains have been examined, and, from the evidence of congested blood, scientists have said they must have died by drowning. And within their stomachs are remains of their last meals: grasses and other plants *utterly foreign to the region.* Various explanations of these finds have been advanced. To many, they certainly seem to be evidence of some sort of cataclysmic change. That they are a product of the Flood seems a distinct possibility.

Once again, let's remember that this is not proof that the Bible is right and "science" wrong. But it is another indication that the biblical picture of the past fits as well as or better than most modern theories. As long as "science" rules out *a priori* the kind of God the Bible reveals, we can expect the unbelieving scientist to struggle to explain his facts within the framework of the physical world. But no Christian, aware that God is, and that He is a rewarder of them who seek Him (Heb. 11:6), ever need apologize for the intellectual *and scientific* respectability of his faith.

9
What's new?

We've all heard the old objection that the Bible contains primitive and unscientific ideas. Ideas like "the world is flat," and "the sun rotates around the earth." Actually, the Bible says no such things. The Bible does speak of the four corners of the earth, which some once interpreted to imply flatness. We also talk of the four corners of the earth in conversation today, though we know very well that the earth is round. (Really, the Bible talks of the "circle of the earth," not it's flatness—Isa. 40:22).

The Bible does talk of the sun rising and moving across the heavens. But after all, modern newspapers daily list the time of "sunrise" . . . and get no ridiculing letters. Everyone realizes what the newspaper is saying, and that "sunrise" is phenomenological language, describing something as it appears to us rather than in the careful and sober terms of scientific explanation.

Ordinary language just isn't scientific language. And the Bible? It doesn't pretend to be a science text. Instead it speaks to people in the language of the ordinary man. And so nearly all the "scientific" objections to its language can be explained.

Now this explanation isn't really a cop out. The Bible admittedly *ought* to speak accurately on matters that concern science when they come up. And it is just here that advances in modern science have proven most interesting.

James Reid
In a 1971 book, *Does Science Confront the Bible?* (Zondervan, $3.95), Reid turns the old arguments around. He points out that the Bible uses words and concepts that make sense in view of the most recent of scientific discoveries, and that were not understandable until our science caught up.

For instance, consider the Hebrews statement that the things which are seen are not made of things which do appear (Heb. 11:3). Have we here a hint of modern atomic physics, which has come to realize that the basic building blocks of the universe are not material at all, but subatomic?

Do descriptions of the heavens dissolving in a fervent heat (2 Peter 3:10) and of massive judgments in Revelation, indicate a coming atomic war? Certainly the pictures there fit the very kind of destruction man now knows can be unleashed by tapping atomic energy—and which no man knew of before our own century.

Dr. Henry Morris in *Studies in Science and the Bible* (Presbyterian and Reformed Publishing Co., $3.50) has written the following:

> All of the energy for maintaining geological (and other) processes must come originally from the sun, and this is recognized in such passages of the Bible as Genesis 1:15, Psalm 19:6, and others. The basic principle of isotasy (meaning "equal weights"), which is the foundation of geophysics, is indicated by Isaiah 40:12, which speaks of God weighing "the mountains in scales and the hills in a balance," from which the preeminent importance of gravitational forces in geophysical calculations should easily be inferred. The "shape of the earth" is the peculiar domain of the subscience of *geodesy,* and the fact of its basic roundness is pointed out in Isaiah 40:22. The rotation of the earth is implied in Job 38:12, 13 as well as other places, and the gravitational field of force in Job 26:7.

Proof?
No. But certainly suggestive. And certainly something that any Christian who is told that his faith is "primitive" and that "modern science" has disproven the Bible will want to know.

But let's remember in all this that arguing our case from science (even though we have a better case than the unbeliever) is unlikely to convert anyone. At best, giving our reasons can clear away any contempt for Christian faith that a distorted concept of science and its findings may sometimes create. When the contempt is cleared away, some will be more ready to listen to what the Bible says about Jesus Christ.

For ultimately, Jesus is the issue. And we are all invited to put the Bible's claims about Him to the most scientific of tests!

10
The test

Science approaches life with a healthy skepticism. At its best (when not defensively attempting to justify its presuppositions against its own evidence) science insists on testing and verifying, on finding out for itself whether claims are false or true.

This is a healthy attitude to carry over to our examination of the Bible. For the Bible makes many striking claims that invite examination by each individual.

First, the Bible's portrait of man is very different from the secular scientist's. Human beings are not the chance products of a blind and mindless universe. We are a direct creation of God, who shaped and formed us for Him to love, and to love Him in return. But man was not responsive to God. Adam and Eve disobeyed, and by the one great mutation Scripture speaks of, mankind was warped out of God's pattern by sin. From that historic date the record of our race has shown in brutal wars and suffering and inhumanity our desperate need to be again what we once were.

But the Bible moves on. God fully understood both the need of men and the only remedy for sin. He took it on Himself to act. Across history God took careful steps: calling the man Abraham; setting aside his children as a special people through which He would communicate with all; finally, through a young Jewish girl, stepping into our world as a human being. The God of the Bible, who had always been free to work in the universe

He created, entered it! And, in the Person of Jesus Christ, God Himself was swung up against the sky to hang on a wooden cross. The Bible says that that death was planned. Planned because it was the only way God could reverse sin's mutation and bring us into harmony with Himself and with each other.

For us

These are drastic claims. We are offered new life, a personal relationship with God, freedom from death's bondage, eternal bliss. *But these are claims that can be verified!* "That which we have seen and heard," a New Testament writer begins, "declare we unto you" (1 John 1:3). This man, through Jesus, experienced fellowship with God. He turns to us and says, in effect, "I am writing to you, so that you may have fellowship with us . . . fellowship with God the Father and His Son Jesus Christ."

Since the days of John, millions of men and women have testified that, through Jesus Christ, they have come to know God. That they have experienced Him; seen Him work in their lives and in their physical surroundings. And these men and women have turned to others with the invitation, "You come, and see."

It's this invitation that is so "scientific," so much in harmony with the scientist's desire to verify for himself what others describe. And it is in just this sense that God encourages us to a "scientific" approach to faith. He encourages each of us to let Him enter our lives, and become real to us.

By this I *don't* mean that a person who is not yet a Christian should, against his will or with mental reservations, say, "All right. I'll try." (Though sometimes God may reach out to such a man and create faith.) No, what I mean is that we should be willing to come to the Word of God with an open mind. We should listen to what God has to say. And we should open our lives to God, and ask Him, *if He is real,* to speak to us and help us hear. Then when the words of Scripture bring us face to face with Him, and we are brought by the Holy Spirit to the point of decision, we can step forward to "taste and see that the Lord is good; blessed is the man that trusteth in Him" (Ps. 34:8).

Come. Find out for yourself.

God is

God is, and God can be known. This faith of the Christian rests, not on arguments from science, but on the testimony of the Word of God, confirmed by his own personal experience. And this, ultimately, is where our discussion must rest. "I know whom I have believed," the Apostle Paul affirms in the Bible. And so today the Christian echoes, "I know. For I know Him."

It's here, in Jesus Christ, and not in little books like this on science or in the arguments of believers or unbelievers, that *your* questions can be answered.

FOR FURTHER READING:

in the Bible: meet Jesus in John's Gospel (New Testament)
on organic evolution: Genes, Genesis, and Evolution (John Klotz, Concordia, $6.95)
on the Flood: The Genesis Flood (Whitcomb and Morris, Baker Book House, $1.95)
on miracles: Miracles (C. S. Lewis, MacMillan, $.95)
on knowing God: Is God Necessary? (Larry Richards, Moody Press, $1.95)